ADHD in Adults

By

Cindy Stringer Wismer

Pearls Publishing House PPH

ISBN-13:978-1499513240

ISBN-10:1499513240

To my son, Harrison- the light of my life.

Table of Contents

Preface

ADHD is not just a childhood problem. If you were diagnosed with ADHD as a child, chances are you have carried some of its symptoms into adulthood. Even if you were not diagnosed as a child, which was a common oversight in the past, you might be dealing with adult ADHD.

Did your parents and teachers label you the class clown, a dreamer, a trouble-maker, or poor student? Maybe you were able to compensate as a child but as adult responsibilities increase the symptoms become more difficult to manage. Managing a career, family, and running a household is a challenge to anyone, but adult ADHD may make it seem impossible.

Adults with ADHD are more likely to change employers more frequently and perform poorly with less job satisfaction. They have more driving violations and are more likely to drop out of school.

While I have used my best efforts in preparing this book, I make no warranties with the respect to the accuracy or completeness of the contents. The advice and strategies contained herein may not be suitable for your situation. You should consult with a professional where appropriate.

Introduction

After teaching for thirty-five years, mostly in the field of special education, I feel compelled to share some of my knowledge with you.

The challenges of adult ADHD can be managed. With the right strategies you can turn your weaknesses into strengths and succeed on your own terms. My hope is that this book will lighten your load and make your journey a little less difficult.

Included in this book are:

-the definition of ADHD

-types of ADHD

-symptoms of ADHD in adults

-comorbid conditions

-treatments for ADHD

-strategies for adults with ADHD

The American Psychiatric Association's Diagnostic and Statistical Manuel, Fifth edition (DSM-5) is used by mental health professionals to diagnose ADHD. Only professionals can diagnose ADHD. This is for information only.

DSM-5 Criteria for Attention Deficit Hyperactive Disorder (ADHD):

People with ADHD show a persistent pattern of inattention and/or hyperactivity-impulsivity that interferes with functioning or development:

1. Inattention: Five or more symptoms of inattention for people 17 and older; symptoms have been present for at least 6 months, and they are inappropriate for developmental level:
   -Often fails to give close attention to details or makes careless mistakes at work or with other activities.
   -Often has trouble holding attention on tasks.
   -Often does not seem to listen when spoken to directly.
   -Often does not follow through on instructions and fails to finish schoolwork, chores, or duties in the workplace (e.g., loses focus, side-tracked).
   -Often has trouble organizing tasks and activities.

-Often avoids, dislikes or is reluctant to do tasks that require mental effort over a long period of time (such as schoolwork).
-Often loses things necessary for tasks and activities (e.g., materials, pencils, books, tools, keys, wallet, paperwork, eyeglasses, and cell phone).
-Is easily distracted
-Is often forgetful in daily activities

2. Hyperactivity and Impulsivity: Five or more symptoms of hyperactivity- impulsivity for people 17 to adults; symptoms have been present for at least 6 months to an extent that is disruptive and inappropriate for the person's developmental level:

-Often fidgets with or taps hands or feet, or squirms in seat.

-Often leaves seat in situations where remaining seated is expected.

-Often feels restless.

-Often unable to take part in leisure activities quietly.

-Is often "on the go" acting as if "driven by a motor."

-Often talks excessively.

-Often blurts out an answer before the question has been completed.

-Often has trouble waiting his/her turn.

-Often interrupts or intrudes on others (e.g., butts into conversations).

In addition, the following conditions must be met:

-Several inattentive or hyperactive- impulsive symptoms were present before age 12.

-Several symptoms are present in two or more settings (e.g., at home, school, work, with friends or relatives; in other activities).

-There is clear evidence that the symptoms interfere with, or reduce the quality of, social, school, or work functioning.

-The symptoms do not happen only during the course if schizophrenia or another psychotic disorder. The symptoms are not better explained by another mental disorder (e.g., Mood Disorder, Anxiety Disorder, Dissociative Disorder, or a Personality Disorder).

According to the DSM-5 there are three types of ADHD:

1. Combined presentation (both hyperactive and inattentive)
2. Predominantly Inattentive presentation (difficulty focusing but not apparently hyperactive)
3. Predominantly Hyperactive- Impulsive presentation (able to focus but hyperactive and impulsive)

Dr. Amen, a psychiatrist who is the medical director of Amen Clinics in California, Washington, and Virginia, uses a combination of symptoms and brain scans to identify six types of ADHD:

1. Classic ADHD
2. Inattentive ADHD
3. Over-focused ADHD- ADHD with negative thoughts and behaviors, opposition, arguing
4. Temporal Lobe ADHD- ADHD with irritability, aggressiveness, memory and learning problems
5. Limbic ADHD- ADHD with depression, low energy and decreased motivation
6. The Ring of Fire- ADHD with Bipolar Disorder, moodiness, aggressiveness and anger

Dr. Amen has studied the effects of medication on each type. He has found that different types respond better to different medications. In my observations of people with ADHD on medication, I have found it often takes trying several medications to find the one that works for you.

A note on the Over Focused ADHD- I have often heard people say they can't be ADHD because they can focus for long periods of time. With Over Focused ADHD you may 'hyper focus' on an interesting activity to the exclusion of everything else. The problem is, not all tasks are interesting. Grocery lists, reading directions, chores must be done. The person with ADHD will put off non-preferred activities and instead focus on preferred activities. When interrupted a person with this type of ADHD will often be irritable.

All adults have symptoms of ADHD on occasion. True Adult ADHD differs in that it is a chronic impairment. It may at times look like a lack of willpower. Some might say, "You are intelligent enough. You just lack the willpower to do the work." However it is not a lack of willpower, but instead a chemical problem in the management systems of the brain. It affects people of all intellects.   Children with ADHD have a 60% likelihood of having some symptoms in adulthood. Four percent of adults have ADHD, and it is not uncommon for it to be undiagnosed. However, if you are diagnosed with ADHD as an adult you did have ADHD as a child. Adults with ADHD are six times more likely to have depression, anxiety, and other psychiatric problems or learning problems.

A friend of mine (John) has many home projects started but very few complete. His wife (Betty) wanted new kitchen cabinets. Two years later the cupboard doors are still in the garage. John had good intentions. He removed the doors and started sanding them, leaving the cupboards with no doors on them. The doors now take up the place where Betty used to park. Finishing jobs is a challenge for John and leads to stress in his relationship. John handles the stress by drinking. Drinking leads to more arguments where

John speaks before he thinks.   John has ADHD and is impulsive;

The impulsivity part of adult ADHD may cause problems with controlling behavior or comments. You may 'act before you think' or 'react without considering the consequences.' Some of the possible symptoms of impulsivity in adult ADHD are:

-poor self-control

-substance abuse or addiction

-struggling to complete tasks

-poor listening skills

-frequently interrupting others or talking over others in conversation

My son's friend, (Dave), is attending college. Dave is very intelligent and definitely college material. He doesn't understand why it is so much harder for him than his friends to complete his assignments on time. Dave finds himself 'zoning out' during lectures. He has been embarrassed when the professor asks him a question he can't answer because he was distracted. Homework is over- whelming. He has to read the text many times to understand, because it is boring to him.

He plays video games for hours at a time. He is able to focus on video games so much that he forgets his other responsibilities. Dave has ADHD. He has difficulty with concentration and focus.

Adults with ADHD may have difficulty with concentration and focus. Completing the daily mundane tasks is difficult. Perhaps you bounce from one activity to another because you are easily bored. Some symptoms of poor concentration and focus related to adult ADHD are:

-zoning out without realizing it (perhaps during a conversation or when your boss is giving you directions)

-difficulty following directions

-overlooking details

-extreme distractibility

-difficulty concentrating when reading (You may have to read a paragraph or page several times to get the meaning.)

I worked with a teacher, (Oliver), who had ADHD. His desk was so messy and cluttered you couldn't see the top of it. Oliver procrastinated on grading students' work. He would wait until report card time and spend an entire weekend grading papers and filling out cards. Oliver taught Computer Science. It would seem logical to use a computer gradebook and enter grades daily. He also had an extremely messy home. He had lost his wallet three times, having to renew his driver's license, cancel and get new credit card, not to mention a new wallet. He was often late for class because he couldn't find his keys. Oliver's ADHD manifested in disorganization and forgetfulness.

If life often seems chaotic and out of control, you may have the disorganization and forgetfulness of adult ADHD. These symptoms often make being organized extremely difficult. You may find it difficult to sort out what is important information relevant to the task at hand. Prioritizing, managing your time, and keeping track of responsibilities is difficult. Some symptoms of disorganization and forgetfulness of adult ADHD are:

-poor organization (home, work, office, desk is messy and cluttered)

-procrastination – Sometimes the task at hand seems so overwhelming you put it off until the last possible moment.

-trouble starting and finishing a project

-chronic lateness

-forgetting appointments, commitments, deadlines

-losing or misplacing things (keys, wallet, phone, documents, bills)

-underestimating the time it will take to complete a task

We all know someone who monopolizes the conversation. (Lisa) talks nonstop about all the details of her life. When you try to contribute to the conversation she often 'over talks' what you are saying. Lisa also fidgets. Her toes are always tapping and she doesn't sit still for long. Lisa is the first one to suggest a trip to Vegas. It doesn't matter that she can't afford it. She craves excitement and is bored much of the time.

Hyperactivity and restlessness in adults with ADHD can look very similar to how it looks in children with ADHD. Or, it may become more subtle as you age. You may be very energetic and always 'on the go.'

Symptoms of hyperactivity and restlessness associated with adult ADHD are:

-agitation- a feeling of an inner restlessness

-risk taking

-easily bored

-racing thoughts

-fidgeting and trouble sitting still

-craving excitement

-excessive talking

My friend (Helen) has worked in many jobs. She told me she feels like a failure because she just can't find a job she likes. Helen begins a new job eager to succeed but quickly becomes moody and irritable. Whenever her boss criticizes her, as bosses tend to do, she comes home crying. I have tried to give her advice but she blames the boss and gets angry. Helen has ADHD with many emotional symptoms.

Difficulty managing frustration can lead to some emotional symptoms in adults with ADHD:

-sense of underachievement

-easily stressed

-irritable

-mood swings

-trouble staying motivated

-very sensitive to criticism

-short or explosive temper

-low self-esteem

Now let's return to Dave, the video game player.

The other side of difficulty focusing is a paradoxical ability to hyper focus. You may become so absorbed in a task that is stimulating or rewarding that you lose track of time and responsibilities. Hyper focusing is thought to be a coping mechanism for distractions, a way of tuning out chaos. If channeled into productive activities the ability to hyper focus can be an asset.

A *comorbid condition* is one or more conditions present in addition to the primary diagnosis- in this case, Adult ADHD.

ADHD is associated with abnormalities in the frontal lobes. Therefore a person with ADHD has increased risk for any neurological condition that originates in these regions. According to the CDC, experts feel that comorbidity is not being properly diagnosed. Comorbid conditions often go untreated. According to the Journal of Psychiatry 87% of adults with ADHD have at least one comorbid condition and 56% of adults with ADHD have at least two comorbid conditions.

Some comorbid disorders commonly found with Adult ADHD are anxiety, depression, mood disorders, learning disorders and OCD (obsessive compulsive disorder). Adults with ADHD are also more likely to abuse alcohol and other substances.

Thirty to seventy percent of children with ADHD will continue to have symptoms that affect adult functioning. Adults diagnosed with ADHD had ADHD as a child, sometimes undiagnosed. In children ADHD affects males more than girls but the ratio evens out in adults, affecting males and females equally. It is thought that 4-5% of adults have ADHD.

Experts believe there is a strong genetic component to ADHD, with certain neurotransmitters in the brain differing in people with ADHD. It tends to run in families. If one parent has ADHD there is a 33% likelihood that their child will also have ADHD. It occurs in people of all intelligences.

In some cases there is no genetic component. ADHD may be caused by:

-smoking and/or drinking while pregnant

-low birth weight

-head injury, especially to the frontal lobes

-exposure to lead, pesticides, or other environmental toxins

ADHD is included in the Americans with Disabilities Act. This means that employers and colleges must make adjustments to address workers' and students' needs.

The struggle of adults with ADHD regarding focus, attention and impulse control affects everyday life. Adults that are unaware that they have ADHD may wonder why they are unable to reach their goals. The inability to focus and follow through can derail careers, ambitions and relationships. Often these people seek help for other disorders such as depression and anxiety and discover they have symptoms of ADHD. For an ADHD diagnosis to be made the symptoms must have been present since childhood. Old report cards or talking to relatives can reveal if hyperactivity or lack of focus were childhood problems.

Once the ADHD diagnosis is made by a health-care professional, interventions and treatments will be decided.

The most common treatment for adults is medication. The same medications that are effective in childhood ADHD are found to be effective in adults. Stimulants are the most prescribed medication. It may seem peculiar that a stimulant is used for ADHD. Stimulants have been found to sharpen concentration by correcting the imbalance of brain chemicals. As the brain becomes more active, the body becomes less active and the person is able to better focus on the required task.

Doctors sometimes also prescribe an anti-depressant to stabilize mood. The decision to use medications for ADHD must be made by a professional.

Even with medications you may struggle with low self-esteem and poor habits. Counseling for ADHD often focuses on getting organized and improving social skills.

The smartphone has apps that can be very helpful in organization. In the evening you can create a to-do list for the next day. You can organize the list into categories such as; calls, emails, tasks, errands. If you aren't comfortable with using an app, make a written list for the next day of what needs to be accomplished. Check off tasks as they are completed. There is also a calendar app where all appointments, birthdays, and important events can be written and readily accessible.

Job coaching by a mentor to help with organization, keeping a daily planner and prioritizing a to-do list will make the transition into the work force much more successful.

A life coach can help you put the newly learned skills into real-life situations.

Colleges also will make adjustments necessary for you to succeed. A school counselor will help to decide what accommodations you need to be successful. Having a note-taker, tutoring, and frequent check-ins with your counselor are services colleges provide.

Having ADHD should not prevent you from having the career you desire. Careers that adults with ADHD seem to find more satisfying are:

-Sales

-Acting

-Military

-Photography

-Trade professions

If you are like most people with ADHD, daily life can seem frustrating and occasionally over whelming. How much time do you waste looking for your keys, wallet, glasses or brief case? Have you arrived at work only to realize you left an important paper, due today, at home? Don't beat yourself up about it. Instead, try some of these strategies for simplifying your life:

-Create a place close to the front door for keys, glasses, wallets and brief cases. **Always** keep these items there. Once you create this habit it will ensure you are out the door on time each morning.

-Buy a colorful wallet, purse, brief case. It will be harder to lose.

-De-clutter- Visual clutter can be over whelming for anybody, but especially so for someone with ADHD. The first step is to stop buying things you don't *really* need. Buy experiences instead of material things. Go to a movie instead of buying a new trinket. I have a friend with a rule: for each new 'thing' that comes into the house one old 'thing' is donated or trashed.

Label four boxes; keep, donate, trash, not yet. Put items in the boxes using the 'not yet' box for items you can't part with yet. Don't agonize over deciding which box to put an item in. If you aren't sure put it in the 'not yet' box and keep going. Come back to the 'not yet' box in a month and reevaluate. Toss those unread magazines.

-Simplify your wardrobe- The less you have the easier it will be to stay organized. It will also be easier to get dressed in the morning if you have fewer choices.

-Set time limits for decision making. People with ADHD have trouble making decisions. You might spend days comparing cell phones, deciding on which summer camp to send your child, or which computer to buy. Set a limit on time to decide and amount of money you can spend.

-Fight hyper focus- Set a timer when you play video games or engage in a preferred activity that you find difficult to stop.

-Enlist help from family members or friends. When doing a mundane task that you find difficult to finish, have a friend or family member sit by you and keep you focused. For example; your wife can sit by you when you are paying bills. She can help by putting the stamps on the envelopes or making sure all bills are paid. She should try to refrain from distracting you.

-Attend a support group

-Use a pill container and fill it once a week.

Chapter 8 – Positives

Though ADHD is a serious disorder it does have some positive aspects. People with ADHD tend to look beyond the norm.

Impulsive behavior may be described as living in the present without putting much thought into tomorrow. Wouldn't we all enjoy having more 'living in the present' moments? They are more likely to try new things without trepidation?

Hyperactivity = high energy which is important in athletics and acting.

ADHD does not slow down the learning process in college if strategies specifically geared towards the learner are used. You can achieve your goals and be successful.

Some of the many successful people with ADHD:

-Sir Richard Branson

-Jim Carrey

-Woody Harrelson

-Howie Mandel

-Pete Rose

-Michael Phelps

-Robin Williams

-Will Smith

-_____ (insert your name here)

And the list goes on and on.

Conclusion

I sincerely hope this book has been helpful for adults with ADHD and their families. With the right strategies and 'life coaches' you **can** be successful. Careers, relationships and home life will be much less stressful with acceptance and understanding, starting with self- awareness.

Please take a few minutes to give this book a review on Amazon and visit me on Facebook @ *Cindy Stringer Wismer author* and *Never Push and Never Pull....a short story*. I am also on Twitter and in Goodreads. I look forward to hearing from you and sharing daily thoughts and information.

Thank you!

A Challenge for **You**

You are reading this book because you, or someone you know, may have adult ADHD. Read again about John, Dave, Oliver, Lisa and Helen. Which strategies would be appropriate for each?

-John, the man who can't seem to finish what he starts. He drinks and argues with his wife.

-Dave, the college student, who zones out in class. He has difficulty studying his boring homework and plays video games for hours.

-Oliver, the school teacher with the cluttered desk and home. He procrastinates. He loses and misplaces items.

-Lisa, the over-talker. She craves excitement and is easily bored.

-Helen has low self-esteem. She bounces from job to job, always blaming the boss. Helen cries easily and gets angry at criticism.

-You.

Sources:

WebMD

Mayo Clinic

John's Hopkins

CDC

Cleveland Clinic

Consumer Health

Guide for Parents

Psychiatric Times

Journal of Psychiatry

www.ingramcontent.com/pod-product-compliance
Lightning Source LLC
Chambersburg PA
CBHW070244290526
45789CB00004B/1758